CROWN

Crystal Renee Thomas

Illustrated by: Ria

www.TrueVinePublishing.org

Copyright page:

Crown
Crystal Renee Thomas

Published by
True Vine Publishing Co.
810 Dominican Dr.
Nashville, TN 37228
www.TrueVinePublishing.org

ISBN: 978-1-962783-59-0 Paperback
ISBN: 978-1-962783-60-6 eBook

Dedication for book is for Jason Jamar Thomas

Giving honor to God who is the head of my life. Without you and your countless blessings, my dreams would not have become a reality. For lifting me up when my faith was at an all-time low, pushing me to pray and to not give up on myself.

To my family for always being in my corner and believing in me and always being my constant means of support. For pushing me when I could no longer push myself.

In a world of uncertainty, I would like to use these affirmations as a steppingstone to promote positivity, greatness and belief in our young black boys. Our boys need to believe that anything is within their reach. And, for them to know that once you get knocked down, you get right back up. Always fight for your beliefs, knowing that all things are possible.

I will Follow God

I will tell all my
testimonies

I will respect my parents

I will be responsible

I am a prince who will become a great king

I will be great
in school

I will be athletic

I will be financially secure

I am strong

I love myself

I am blessed

I can be anything I want to be

The End

www.ingramcontent.com/pod-product-compliance
Lightning Source LLC
Chambersburg PA
CBRC091630140626
46547CB00028B/648

9 781962 783590